Volcanoes

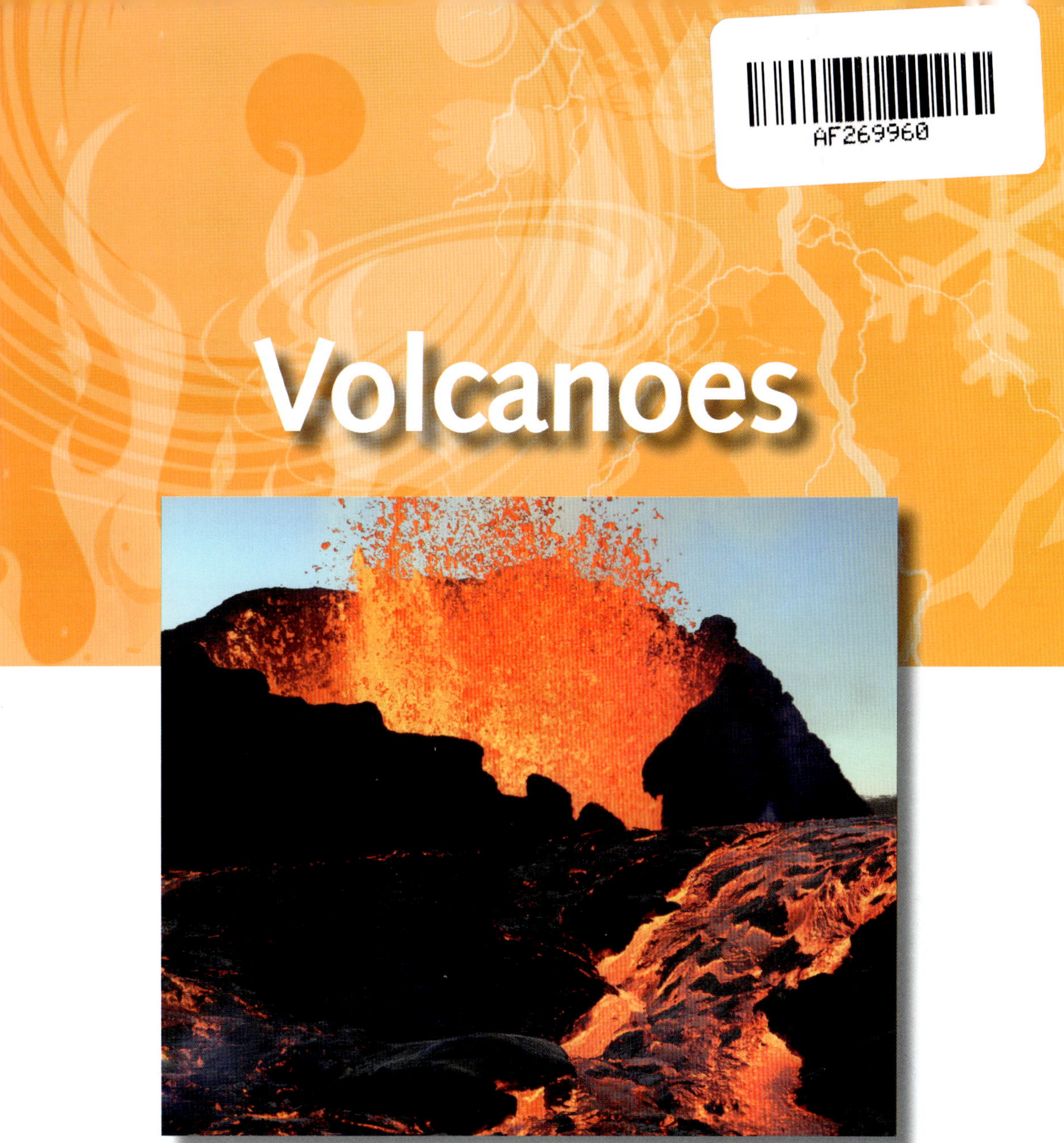

William B. Rice

Volcanoes

Publishing Credits

Associate Editors
James Anderson
Torrey Maloof

Editorial Director
Dona Herweck Rice

Editor-in-Chief
Sharon Coan, M.S.Ed.

Creative Director
Lee Aucoin

Illustration Manager
Timothy J. Bradley

Publisher
Rachelle Cracchiolo, M.S.Ed.

Science Consultant

Scot Oschman, Ph.D.

Teacher Created Materials
5301 Oceanus Drive
Huntington Beach, CA 92649-1030
http://www.tcmpub.com
ISBN 978-1-4333-0310-4
© 2010 Teacher Created Materials Publishing, Inc.
Printed in Malaysia
THU001.50393

Table of Contents

Pressure 4

What Makes a Volcano? 6

Where Do Volcanoes Happen? 14

What Happens During an Eruption? 20

Volcanoes Everywhere 26

Appendices 28

    Lab: Pangea Puzzle 28

    Glossary 30

    Index 31

    Scientists Then and Now 32

    Image Credits 32

Pressure

You are unloading groceries from the car. All of a sudden, a can of soda drops to the ground. It hits the ground hard and then rolls down the driveway. You run to catch it. But you end up kicking it by accident. It crashes into a brick wall. Clunk!

What if you decided to open that can of soda? It was shaken up pretty badly. The gas in the soda has created a lot of **pressure** inside the can. What will happen?

You pop the top and find out. Whoosh! The soda shoots out of the can and overflows down the sides. In other words, it **erupts**. Just like a volcano.

Vulcan

The word *volcano* comes from *Vulcan*. Vulcan is the Roman god of fire.

What Is a Volcano?

A volcano is any place on a planet where material from the inside makes its way to the surface of the planet.

What Makes a Volcano?

Volcanoes erupt every day all over the planet. Some never stop erupting! Some erupt for months and years. Some erupt quickly and then stop just as quickly.

To erupt means to release pressure. Everything that is under pressure is let go. If there is a lot of pressure, the eruption puts on quite a show.

What makes the pressure build beneath a volcano? Earth is not like a soda can. No one shakes it or kicks it against a wall. No one has to. There is a lot going on below Earth's surface. Things are always on the move. This movement builds the pressure.

What causes the movement? There is more than one answer to that question. But one important answer is **plate tectonics**.

Volcanologists

Scientists who study volcanoes are called **volcanologists** (vol-kuh-NOL-uh-jists). Volcanologists study volcanoes on the surface of Earth and beneath it.

How Many?

Scientists think that about 15 volcanoes on Earth erupt each day.

Some volcanoes like these erupt almost all the time. Others sleep, or lie dormant, for years and years. They may never erupt again.

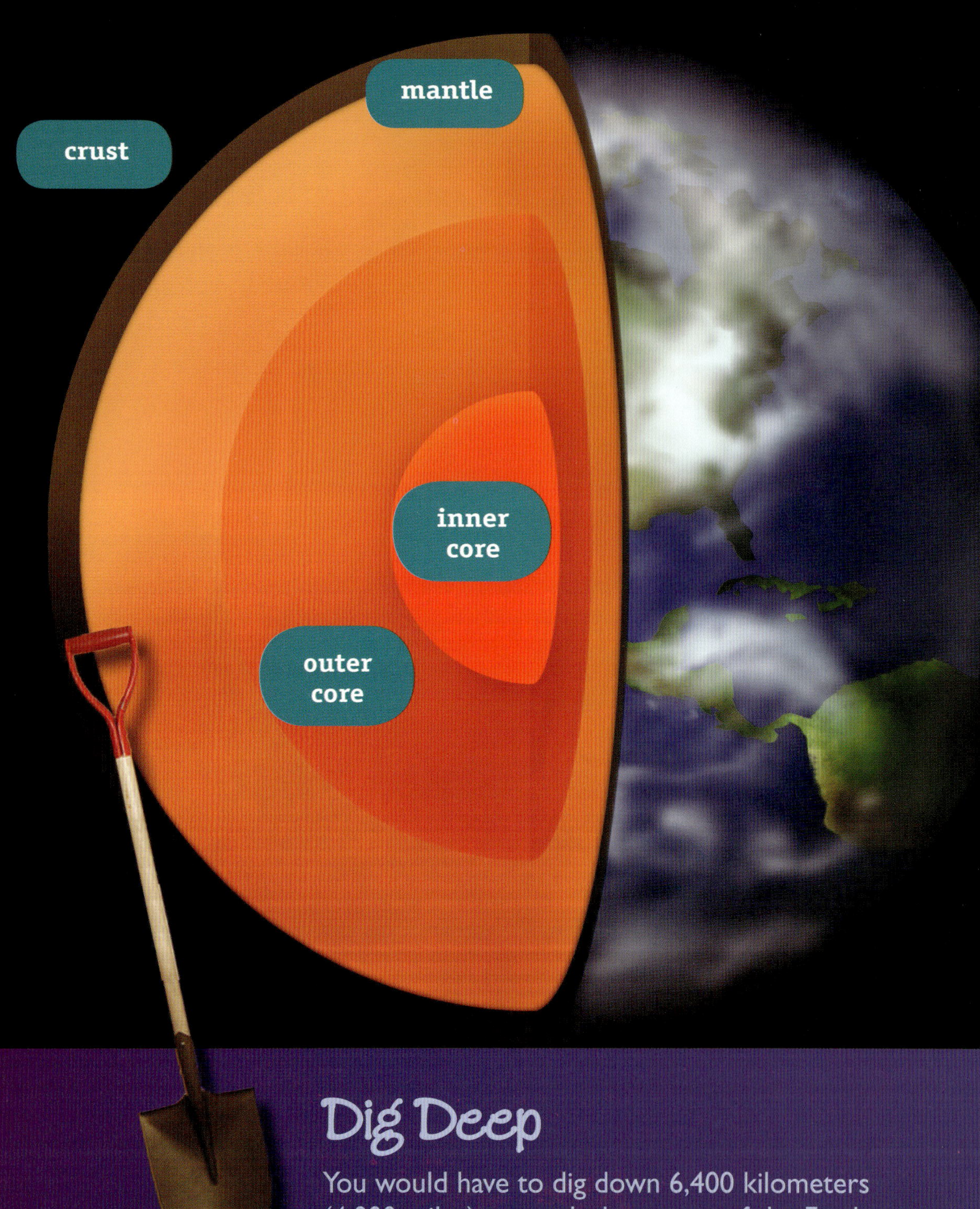

Dig Deep

You would have to dig down 6,400 kilometers (4,000 miles) to reach the center of the Earth.

Plate Tectonics

Earth's outer layer, the **crust**, is not one solid, smooth piece. It is broken up into many large pieces. Each piece is called a **plate**. The plates are made of Earth materials such as rocks and minerals. Some plates are bigger than continents. Some plates are smaller, like a country. Either way, plates are really big.

Earth is made of four main layers. They are the crust, **mantle**, outer core, and inner core. Plates are found in the crust and the top of the mantle. The crust is firm but easily broken. It sits on top of the mantle. The mantle is fluid. It can bend, shift, and flow more easily than the crust can.

The crust (black) makes up less than one percent of the Earth. The core (red) makes up more than 31 percent. The mantle (yellow) makes up about 68 percent.

An Ap-peel-ing Fact

Earth's crust is about 44 kilometers (70 miles) thick in its thickest places. This is not very thick at all when you compare it to the whole planet. It is like the thickness of an apple peel when you compare it to the whole apple.

The mantle is the largest layer. It is very, very hot. It is lucky for living things that the crust covers the mantle. They could not live on the mantle's high heat.

Many people think the mantle is liquid because it is so hot. But even though it is very hot, it is mainly solid. It is a moveable, bendable solid, though. Think of it as something like play clay or very thick glue. It is solid, but it flows. Pressure inside the Earth keeps it solid. It does not usually melt. But sometimes it does. When it melts, it forms **magma**. Magma is hot, liquid rock. It comes up through Earth's crust to the surface.

Earth's plates float on top of the mantle. As the mantle flows, the plates float along as well. They rub against each other as they float. Their movement against each other and the mantle is the main reason why magma is formed.

How Fast Do Plates Move?

Plates move about two and one-half centimeters (one inch) per year. This means that plates can move two and one-half million centimeters (one million inches) in a million years. That is about 25 kilometers (15.5 miles).

On the left is rock formed from magma. On the right is an illustration showing the movement of magma from the mantle to the Earth's suface.

About Magma

Magma is formed under the ground. It is formed in the upper part of the mantle and the lower part of the crust. It takes very high heat and just the right amount of pressure to make magma. The right heat and pressure often happen at the edges of plates. These edges are called **boundaries**.

Magma is lighter than the rock around it. This makes it move upward. It moves through cracks and other openings. It erupts when it reaches the surface.

Magma is mainly liquid. But not all of it is. That is because magma is made of different types of rock. The rocks have their own melting points. Think of a rock made of ice, chocolate, and sugar. Under heat, the ice melts first. Then the chocolate melts. If the heat is not high enough, the sugar may not melt. That is just like the different rocks that melt (or do not melt) to make magma.

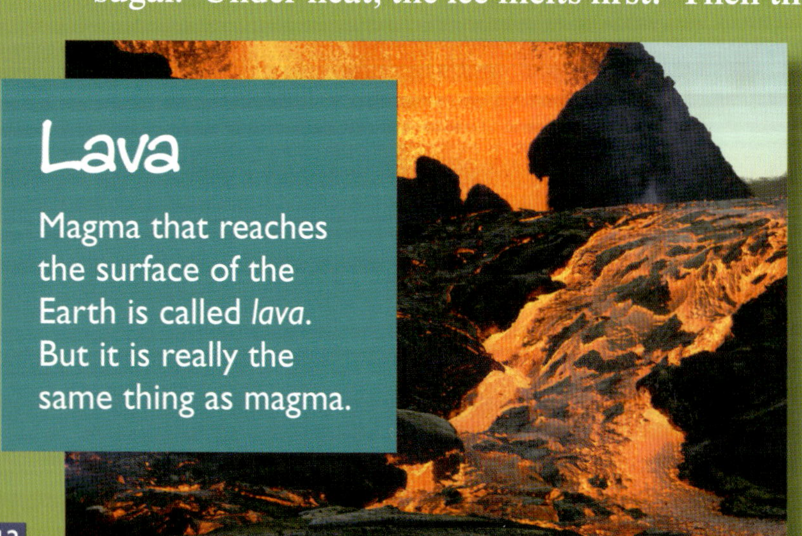

Lava

Magma that reaches the surface of the Earth is called *lava*. But it is really the same thing as magma.

Magma is molten rock. It is hot and mainly liquid. It is also part solid and part gas.

From Magma to Igneous Rock

Igneous rock forms from completely melted rock. The melted rock cools and becomes a solid. The most common igneous rock to form from magma is basalt (buh-SAWLT).

columns of basalt

Underwater

Most volcanoes form under the ocean. They form at spreading centers.

Iceland

Most of the Mid-Atlantic Ridge is underwater. But some is above sea level. For example, the island country of Iceland is formed by the Mid-Atlantic Ridge.

Where Do Volcanoes Happen?

Volcanoes form only in some places. Most form at plate boundaries. Others form within plates over areas called **hot spots**.

Plates keep moving. They move slowly, but they still move. In this way, plates do one of four things. They spread apart, strike, crumple, or move past one another. Volcanoes form in three of these places.

Plate Boundaries

When plates spread apart, they form a ridge. It is a **continental ridge** if the two plates spreading apart are on land. It is a **mid-ocean ridge** if the two plates spreading apart are under the ocean. As the plates pull apart, mantle rock flows up to fill the space. The rock becomes magma. At the surface, the magma cools. It becomes new crust. This is called **spreading center volcanism** (VOL-kuh-niz-uhm).

When plates collide, one of two things happens. The first is that one plate may be pushed under the other plate. The bottom plate sinks into the mantle. A **trench** is formed where the plates meet. Magma forms as the lower plate dives into the mantle. Some of the magma rises. That is where a volcano erupts. It is called **subduction zone volcanism**.

The plates may also crumple into each other. This happens when neither plate can subduct under the other one. The crust of both plates crumples. The plates push up mountains in this way. But they do not make volcanoes.

Plates may also slide past each other. They do not pull apart or push. A volcano may form as they slide. But most of the time, a volcano will not form.

Mount St. Helens

Mount St. Helens in the United States is one of the most famous subduction zone volcanoes in the world.

What Does It Mean?

To *subduct* means to go under something else. When plates subduct, one plate goes under the other plate.

Here is Mount St. Helens before (upper left), during (center), and after its 1980 eruption (above).

Volcanoes can also form at hot spots. Hawaii was made in this way. Hawaii is made of many islands. They have formed over a long time. But Hawaii is far from a plate boundary.

A hot spot is a very hot area below the plate. Magma pushes through the crust at this spot. As more magma pushes through, it forms a volcano. The volcano grows over time. In the ocean, the volcano and lava form an island.

New volcanoes and islands form as the plate moves over the hot spot. That is why Hawaii is a string of islands. More islands may form over time. The oldest islands may be washed away.

A Lot of Road

Kilauea (kee-lou-EY-h) is a volcano in Hawaii. All the lava that has come from Kilauea can pave a road that wraps three times around Earth!

Old and Young Rock

The oldest rock is farthest away from the hot spot. The oldest island in Hawaii is 5.5 million years old. The youngest island is still over the hot spot. It is less than one million years old.

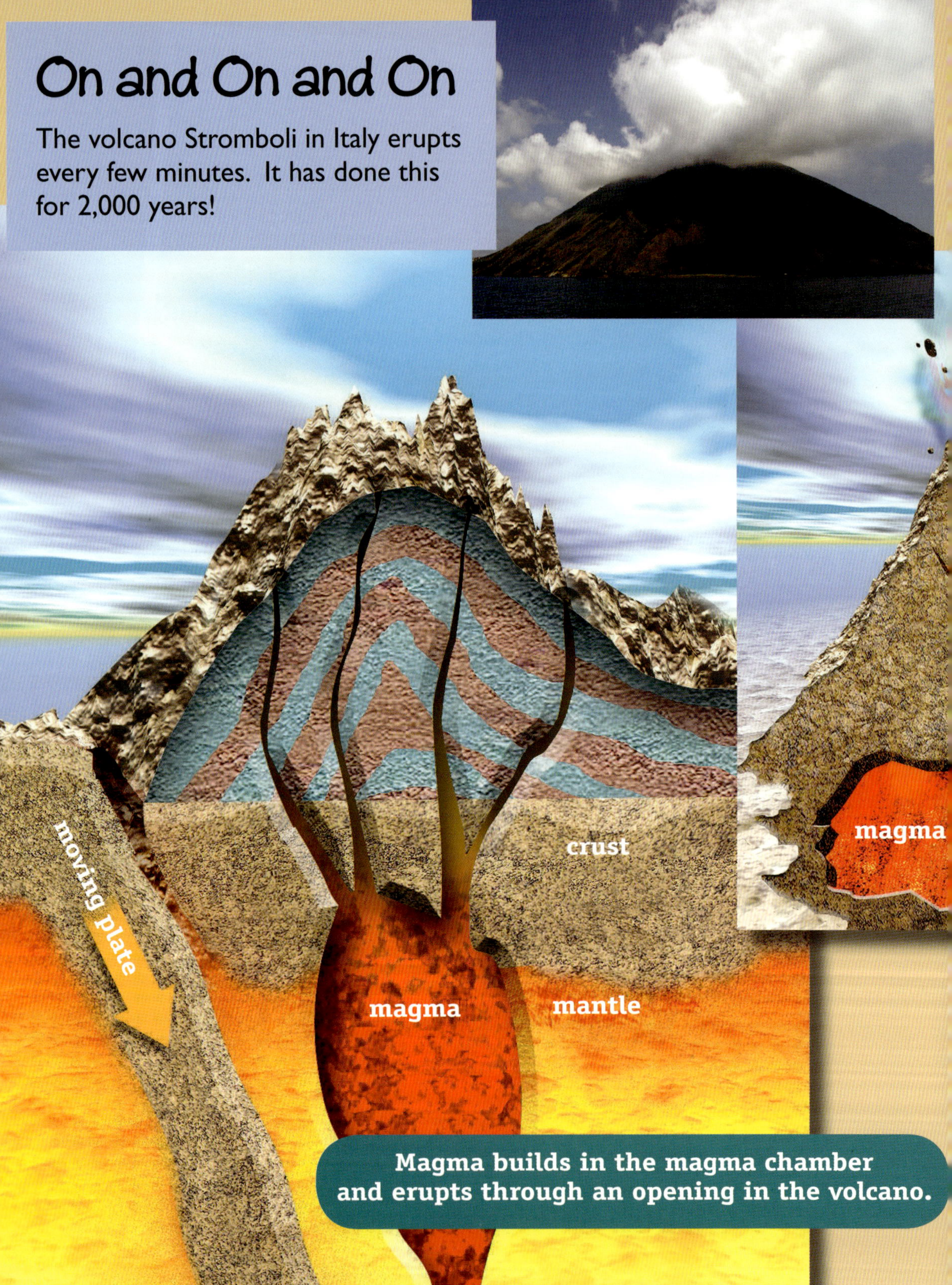

On and On and On

The volcano Stromboli in Italy erupts every few minutes. It has done this for 2,000 years!

Magma builds in the magma chamber and erupts through an opening in the volcano.

What Happens During an Eruption?

All eruptions do not look the same. But they do have things in common.

Pressure and heat in the mantle begin an eruption. They push magma into a chamber. Magma is lighter than the crust. So it tries to push above it. And pressure from gases pushes the magma through the crust. When pressure builds, ash, rock, gas, and steam escape. They push through a hole or crack in the Earth. This is an eruption.

Sometimes an eruption comes in a blast. It can be loud like an explosion. Sometimes it comes in a slow ooze. The more pressure, the bigger the blast.

Active, Dormant, or Extinct?

If a volcano might erupt any time, it is called active. If we think it will not erupt now but perhaps in the future, it is called dormant (DOR-muhnt). *Dormant* means *asleep*. If we think it will never erupt, it is called extinct.

Ash, Lapilli, and Bombs

The smallest pieces of lava that come from a volcano are called *ash*. Pieces the size of pebbles and small rocks are called *lapilli*. The largest pieces are called *bombs*. They can be as big as a car!

Magma is called lava when it is outside a volcano. Lava is super hot. It can be fast and runny or slow and thick. Lava pours from the top of a volcano and runs down its sides. Thick lava does not go far. It stops and forms rocks. Some even cools and stops when it is still magma on its way out of the volcano.

The heat of lava will kill most living things. Animals and plants from long ago are sometimes found in old, cooled lava. They become "frozen" in time.

Lava that has erupted may cool quickly. It may cool in just a few days. But it also might take years to cool!

Ring of Fire

There are hundreds of volcanoes around the world. But more than half of them are along the shores of the Pacific Ocean. They are known as the Ring of Fire.

There is some lava in Mexico that is still hot almost 50 years after it was released from the volcano.

We can often tell when a volcano is going to erupt. A full magma chamber makes a volcano bulge. There may be earthquakes. There may be gas fumes, too. The smell of sulfur fills the air. Most of the time, an eruption is not a surprise.

An eruption can last just a few seconds. But it can also last for years and years. Something must happen to make it stop. It will stop when there is no more magma. It will stop when there is not enough gas in the magma. Or it will stop when lava cools and plugs the opening. Of course, the same volcano may erupt again.

Can Water Stop an Eruption?

Water can stop lava from flowing. But it cannot stop a volcano from erupting. Water in a volcano will become steam. The steam will build up pressure and cause the volcano to explode.

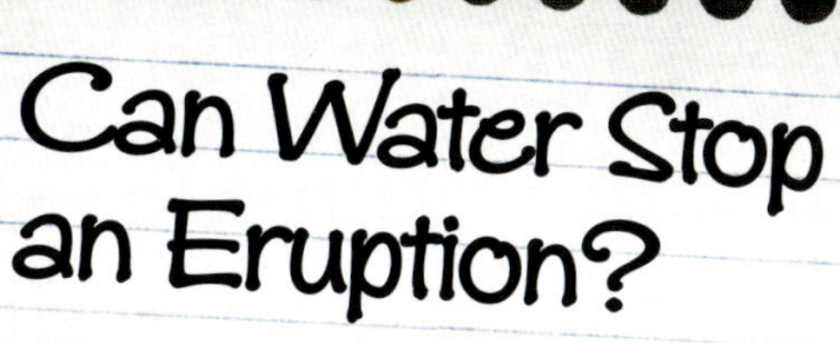

VEI

The Volcanic Explosivity Index (VEI) measures the power of an eruption. It is a scale from 0 to 8. Eight is the most powerful score. The VEI records the eruption's height, how long it lasts, and the amount of material released. All of this information makes up the score. At left is how some famous eruptions scored.

Volcano	Year	VEI Score
Kilauea	1983–present	1
Mount St. Helens	1980	5
Mount Tambora	1815	7

Olympus Mons
on Mars
The Sun
Mars
Earth

Volcanoes Everywhere

Earth is not the only place where volcanoes can be found. They are on other planets, too. The largest volcano we know of is on Mars. It is called Olympus Mons. It is 26 kilometers (16 miles) tall. It is three times as tall as Mount Everest. It is as wide as the state of Arizona!

Volcanoes are one big reason why a planet changes. Many people in history have feared them. They thought volcanoes were caused by the anger of the gods. But we know that volcanoes are part of a planet's growth. It looks like Earth's volcanoes will erupt for a long time to come.

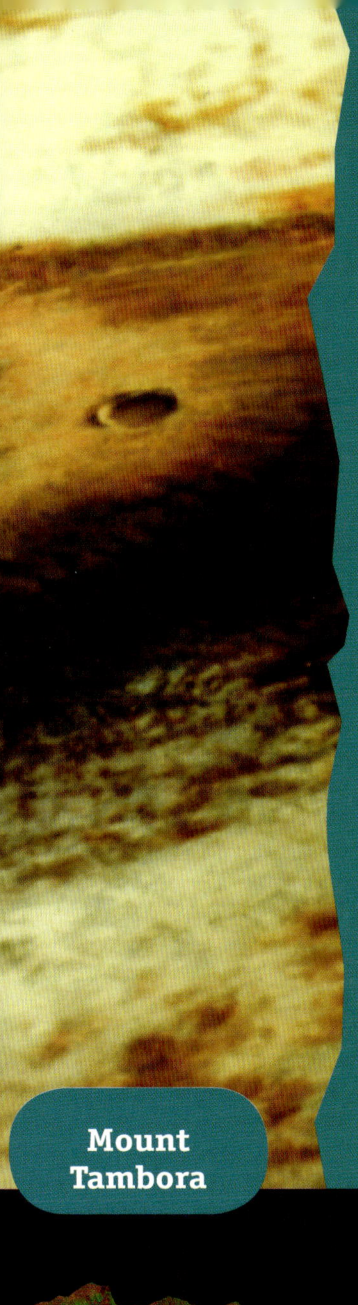

Mount Tambora

Most Powerful Eruption

The most powerful eruption known took place in 1815 in Indonesia. It was Mount Tambora. The eruption shot about 150 cubic kilometers of ash into the air. Ash shot as high as 44 kilometers (28 miles) and landed as far as 1,290 kilometers (800 miles) away. More than 100,000 people were killed. About 82,000 died afterwards of hunger and disease.

Lab: Pangea Puzzle

The theory of plate motion, also called continental drift, was first suggested not very long ago. Scientists saw that the continents seemed to fit together like a puzzle. Along with other evidence, this made them think that perhaps all the continents had once been part of a large land mass called Pangea.

Today we know a lot about plate movement. Pangea seems quite possible. Do this activity to check it out for yourself.

Materials

- a copy of the continents on the next page
- scissors

Procedure:

1. Make a copy of the continents on the next page. You will probably want to enlarge them.

2. Cut out the continents.

3. Try putting the pieces of the continents together as if they were a puzzle.

Conclusion:

Does Pangea seem likely to you? Do the pieces seem to fit together? Research to learn more about Pangea and continental drift.

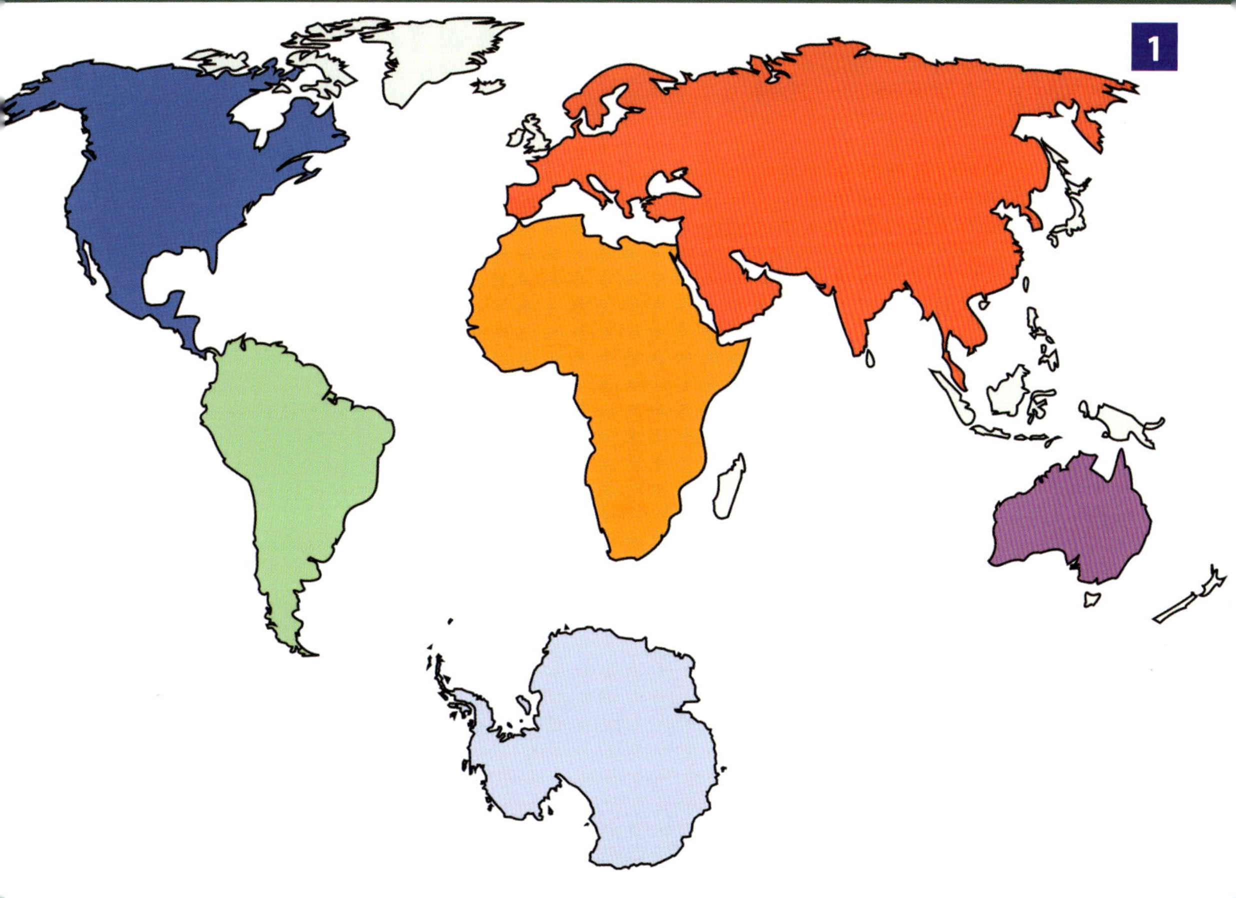

1

2

Glossary

boundary—edge, border, or limit

continental ridge—a ridge formed on land where two plates spread apart

crust—the solid, brittle, upper layer of Earth

erupt—to release pressure; to explode

hot spot—a place inside a tectonic plate that is thin enough for magma to push through and for a volcano to form

magma—hot, soft molten rock

mantle—the hot, molten layer of Earth below the crust

mid-ocean ridge—a ridge formed under the ocean where two plates spread apart

plate—a section of Earth's crust

plate tectonics—the theory that large plates of earth material in the upper layers of the planet move and collide to form the surface features of the Earth

pressure—the exertion of force upon a surface by an object, fluid, or other source in contact with it

spreading center volcanism—creation of a volcano in a place where two plates spread apart

subduction zone volcanism—creation of a volcano in a place where one plate subducts (moves under) another plate

trench—a ditch

volcanologist—a scientist who studies volcanoes

Index

boundary, 12, 15, 18

continental ridge, 15

crust, 8–10, 12, 15–16, 18, 20–21

erupt, 4–7, 12, 16–17, 20–22, 24–27

Hawaii, 18–19

hot spot, 15, 18–19

Kilauea, 19, 25

lava, 12, 18–19, 21–25

magma, 10–13, 15–16, 18, 20–22, 24

mantle, 8–12, 15–16, 20–21

Mid-Atlantic Ridge, 14

Mount St. Helens, 16–17, 25

Mount Tambora, 25, 27

ocean ridge, 15

plate, 6, 9–12, 15–18, 20, 28

pressure, 4–6, 10, 12, 21, 25

Ring of Fire, 23

spreading center volcanism, 15

subduction zone volcanism, 16

trench, 16

Volcanic Explosivity Index, 25

Scientists Then and Now

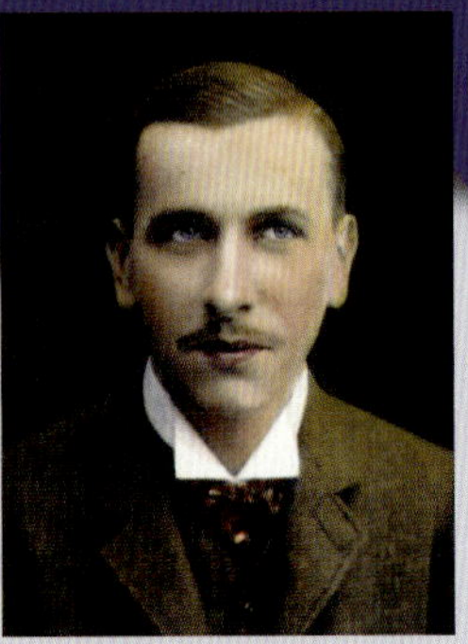

Alfred Wegener
(1880–1930)

Tanya Atwater
(1944–)

Alfred Wegener was an astronomer at first. But one day, the continents caught his interest. He noticed the coastlines. He thought they looked like puzzle pieces. Wegener developed a theory called continental drift. The theory says that the continents were once attached but broke apart and drifted away over time. Wegener's theory led to the study of plate movement, called plate tectonics.

Tanya Atwater is a professor and a scientist. She loves the natural world, and she wants others to love it, too. That is why she teaches. She hopes that she can teach others to respect and care for the planet. Atwater especially studies plate tectonics. Sometimes, she takes a submersible boat all the way to the ocean floor to study sea floor spreading up close!

Image Credits